CONTENTS

Introduction

I'm hoping that my love of experimenting with different fabrics and mediums will shine through the pages of this book.

Everyone is aware that playing is the only way to really learn and quite often you will happen upon those serendipity moments. Personally, I think that playing without a finished project in mind is absolutely the best route to take and, quite often, the samples will 'speak' to you and suggest what to create with that particular technique.

I generally make all my samples into postcard size (or just slightly larger) pieces with finished edges, occasionally backing them with watercolour paper to make them look neater. Sometimes a sample can take on a totally different look once it has been tidied up.

The details of exactly which materials and mediums I have used are then written, either on the back or on a label attached at the edge. This is really helpful. There's nothing more frustrating than finding a gorgeous sample in a box several months later and not being able to remember exactly what you used or how you achieved it!

I also keep all the samples I make, even the ones that didn't turn out quite as well as I had hoped. You just never know when you might have a use for them in the future. I hope you'll enjoy perusing the pages of this book as much as I've enjoyed sharing my sample-making with you.

> Steampunk jacket and flying hat with steampunk goggles. Made using the basic Tyvek and Kunin/acrylic felt technique. The Tyvek was coloured with walnut ink, sprinkled with salt. Watered-down Quinacridone Nickel Azo Gold acrylic paints were then splashed on top.

∨ Steampunk style cuffs made using painted Tyvek bonded to coloured felt.

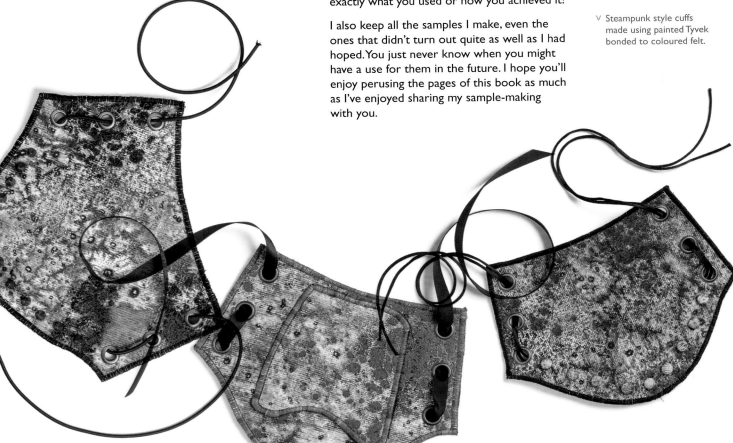

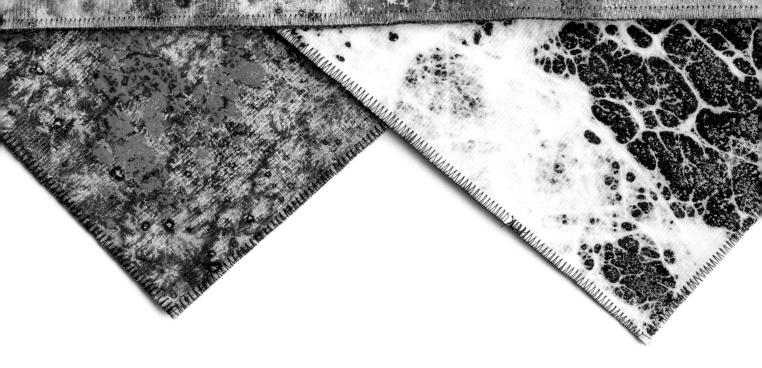

SECTION I
The basics

∧ Samples using the basic
Tyvek technique.

Just three main ingredients are needed for this technique: Tyvek fabric or paper, fusible webbing such as Bondaweb, and Kunin or acrylic felt. By adding various other materials and mediums, the technique can then be taken to the next level.

The resulting fabric can be used as a background and further enhanced with stitch or embellishments. It's also good for book covers, vessels, wearable art and more.

Tyvek

Tyvek, a synthetic material produced from high-density polyethylene fibres, is available as a fabric or three different weights of paper. The fabric variety is not woven but has a softer drape than the paper and is easier to stitch. When heat is applied, the paper will bubble and blister, whereas the fabric will distort with the heat.

The fabric version of Tyvek is the most suitable for this particular technique. A lot of people don't like the appearance of distressed Tyvek at all, whether the paper or the fabric variety. However, used in conjunction with various other fabrics, you can get some really fascinating results.

Kunin felt and acrylic felt

Kunin felt is a polyester fibre made from recycled plastic bottles. It is most often used for burning and distressing techniques. Acrylic felt is much denser than Kunin felt and using this technique will result in a sturdier created fabric. It is ideal for vessels and other three-dimensional work.

∧ The fabric will not fray so it is ideal for use in construction techniques, especially those involving die-cutters.

∨ A selection of buttoned cuffs using the basic method. Here the Tyvek has been coloured using different mediums.

For a trial sample:

1. I recommend practising with small samples to get the technique right and the iron at the right temperature. These photographs show unpainted Tyvek so that you can see the effect more clearly. Take a piece of Kunin felt or 100% acrylic felt of any colour and lay it on your ironing surface, which will have already been protected with a layer of baking paper.

2. Cut a piece of Bondaweb, or similar fusible webbing, the same size as the felt. Peel the webbing, the adhesive side, from the backing paper. Lay this on top of the felt. Do not iron in place.

3. Cut a piece of Tyvek fabric just a fraction larger than the felt as it will shrink slightly when heated and you want to make sure your edges are covered. If you feel a piece of Tyvek fabric carefully, you will find that one side is soft and the other side has a shiny surface. Place the fabric on top of the felt with the shiny surface facing you. Don't worry if you forget to do this as it will still give you a good result. It's just that the Tyvek fabric tends to shrink more readily if the shiny side is uppermost.

4. Now cover the sandwich with baking paper or similar to protect your iron. Start with your iron on almost the hottest setting. It is impossible to tell you exactly how hot to have your iron as they all differ slightly and it will be a question of trial and error before you find the setting that works best for you. If the Tyvek melts too quickly then turn the iron down a notch. However, if it takes a long time to work then turn the iron up.

5. For larger pieces, always start in the centre at the top of your fabric. The Tyvek fabric will creep slightly as you apply pressure, more so with larger pieces, so start in the centre and work your way out to each edge. Press down really hard with the iron and, in one smooth, slow movement, bring the iron down the fabric, making sure to keep the pressure on until you reach the bottom. Do not linger in one spot for too long or the Tyvek fabric may disappear completely. You can always lift the baking paper and have a look at what is happening. If the Tyvek hasn't melted enough for your liking then just run the iron down the surface again, but more quickly this time as the fabric will still be warm and will melt more readily.

6. Now repeat this process down the left- and the right-hand sides of the fabric.

Very carefully, go over any areas that you don't think have melted back enough. There is a fine line between not having melted enough of the Tyvek and suddenly having nothing left. If you look at the back, you will find it has crinkled in places. Cover with baking paper and iron with the hot iron for a few seconds to help flatten the piece. Don't iron for too long or the heat may travel through the fabric and melt back the Tyvek.

That's the test sample created. Now let's see how we can expand on this technique.

Coloured Tyvek

Tyvek can be coloured in a variety of ways, as you can see.

Colouring the Tyvek beforehand gives a whole new dimension to this technique.

Many types of water-soluble colouring mediums can be used. These include Brusho, ScolaBrush, diluted silk paints or fabric paints, walnut ink, Procion dyes (without any fixatives, or try using spent dye) and diluted acrylic paints.

The acrylic paints must be diluted for several reasons: if they are applied too thickly, it inhibits the Tyvek from melting properly and they tend to leave a very shiny surface on the Tyvek that remains. Finally, and most importantly, they may produce nasty fumes.

Don't apply really dark colours unless that is the type of finish you are after, as the colour may deepen even more once the Tyvek shrinks. Use a wide brush or a sponge to apply the colour.

Metallic paints are ineffectual. The heat of the iron tends to dull the metallic sheen.

> *Painted Tyvek. From top:*

Walnut ink, sea salt, Procion dye

Walnut ink, sea salt, Procion dye and acrylic paint

Acrylic paint – one colour

Quink ink and sea salt

Acrylic paint – multi-coloured

Using gouache can give a different look, similar to craquelure. Bear in mind that when used with Kunin felt, as opposed to acrylic felt, the resulting fabric can be really stretchy and tends to pull out of shape very easily when stitched.

Although the shiny side tends to melt slightly more quickly with some colourings such as Quink writing ink and walnut ink, it may be best to use the soft side as there is a tendency for the colour to lift off, especially in damp conditions.

A sprinkling of sea salt over walnut ink or Procion dye colour can look really effective. It will take slightly longer for the colours to dry if salt is used – and do make sure you brush all of the salt away before use as salt retains moisture.

Try this:

1. Colour with walnut ink.

2. Add the salt.

3. Dip your brush in Procion dye.

4. Splash it on the surface at random.

The result will be a really lovely surface.

∧ Gouche with black Quink writing ink sprayed on surface.

∧ These notepad folios were made using Tyvek coloured with Quink writing ink, acrylic paints and Procion dyes. Some are fastened with poppers and some with covered buttons.

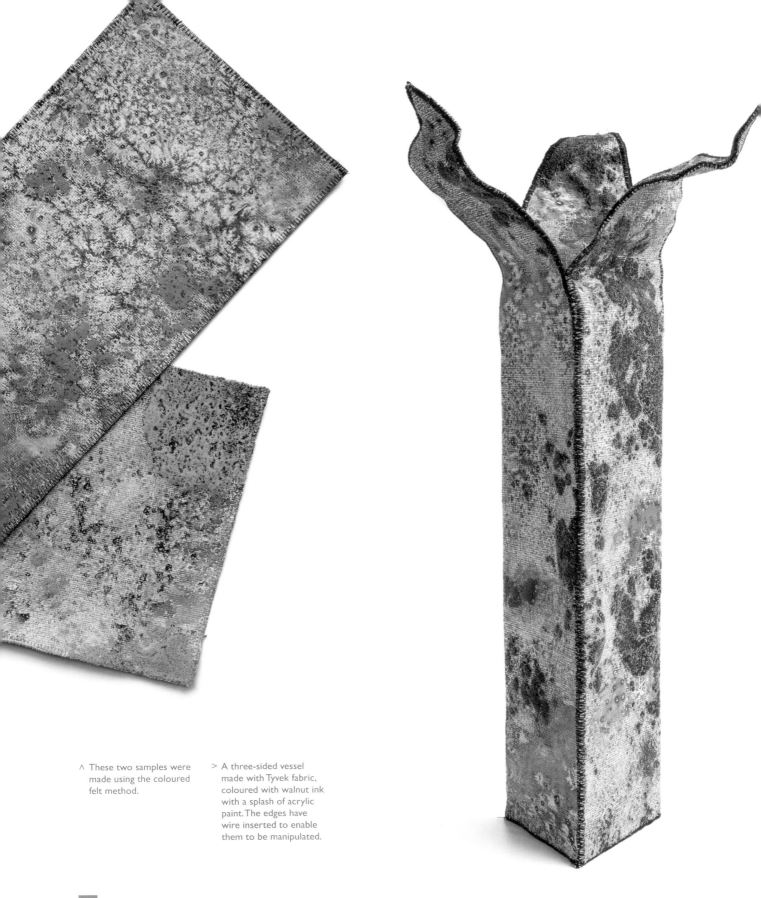

∧ These two samples were made using the coloured felt method.

> A three-sided vessel made with Tyvek fabric, coloured with walnut ink with a splash of acrylic paint. The edges have wire inserted to enable them to be manipulated.

Coloured felt

Any colour felt can be used, depending on the finished look you wish to obtain. For your first few samples, make sure that the felt you use is Kunin or acrylic felt.

White acrylic or Kunin felt can always be coloured with heat transfer dyes.

> The cuffs above show the difference that the background colour (in this case red and blue felt) makes to the finished item.

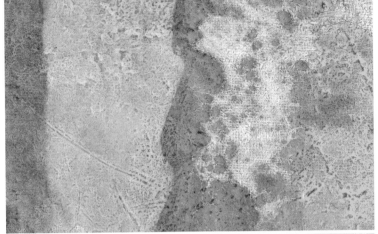

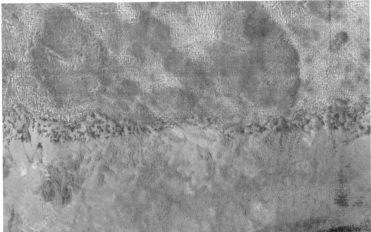

Heat transfer dyes (disperse dyes)

Synthetic fabrics, such as Kunin and acrylic felt, can be successfully coloured with transfer dyes, giving you a whole range of shades and tones rather than using the manufactured flat coloured felt available.

Heat transfer dyes come in the form of crayons, paints and a powdered dye known as disperse dye or transfer dye. You can paint or draw these dyes on paper and use a hot iron or heat press to transfer them to the fabric.

Use printer or copier paper as the substrate on which to paint the dyes. You need an inexpensive paper that will not absorb the liquid colour. Use a wide brush or a foam brush to apply the disperse dye.

When the papers are dry, place them on the felt, colour side down, cover with baking paper and use a hot iron to transfer the print. Move the iron slowly across the paper, otherwise you may get an impression of the iron on the fabric, complete with holes if you use a steam iron! Lift the edge of the paper to see if it is transferring and keep ironing until you are pleased with the result. Why not colour your felt and Tyvek to coordinate or contrast?

> **HINT:** *Once your coloured papers are exhausted, instead of binning them, why not glue two pages together, with the colour on the outside, cover both sides with acrylic wax and then origami-fold them into a 'Grandma's Boasting Book'. You can machine stitch around the edges to make them look tidy and to protect against wear and tear, and stitch embellishments on the front cover.*

< Samples of white felt that have been coloured using disperse dye with coloured Tyvek fabric.

> Transfer-dyed white felt with plain white Tyvek fabric.

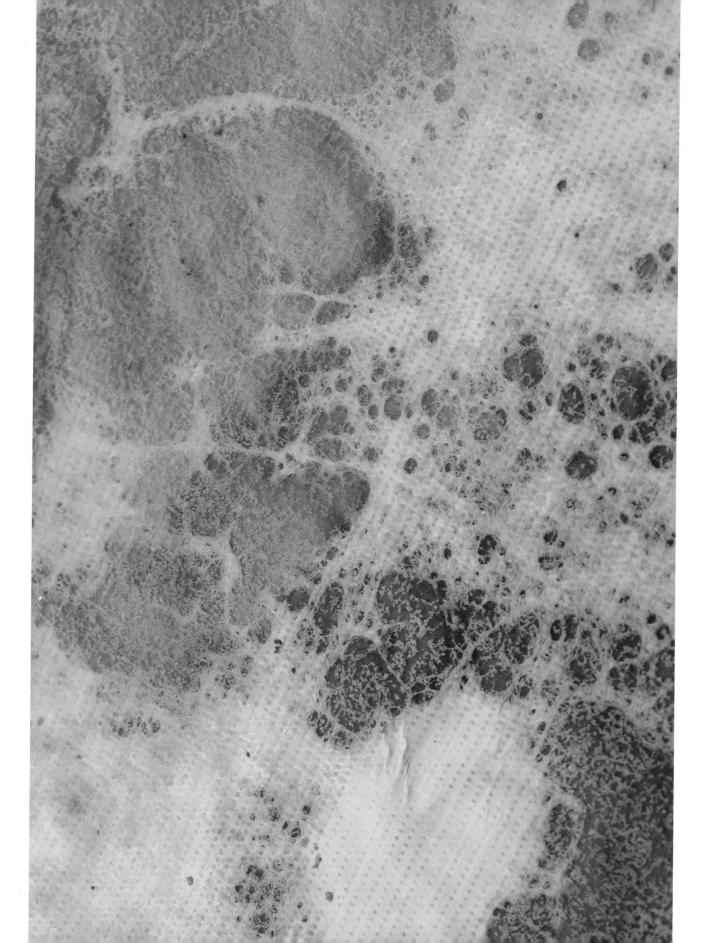

SECTION 2
Moving on

Now to experiment with other mediums. Why not try adding sparkle?

Use glitter flakes to add a bit of sparkle underneath the Tyvek. Just sprinkle the glitter flakes quite liberally onto the felt, cover with the fusible webbing followed by the Tyvek and the baking paper and melt in the usual way with the iron.

You may find that some of the flakes that peep out from the gaps in the Tyvek will be loose. You could rectify this by adding a further layer of webbing underneath the flakes as well as on top, or the melted surface could be covered with organza, net or something similar, all depending on how you plan to use the finished sample.

∧ Heaped glitter flakes with a sample showing the effect when glitter flakes are sprinkled on top of the felt before melting the Tyvek fabric.

> Plague Doctor Masks.

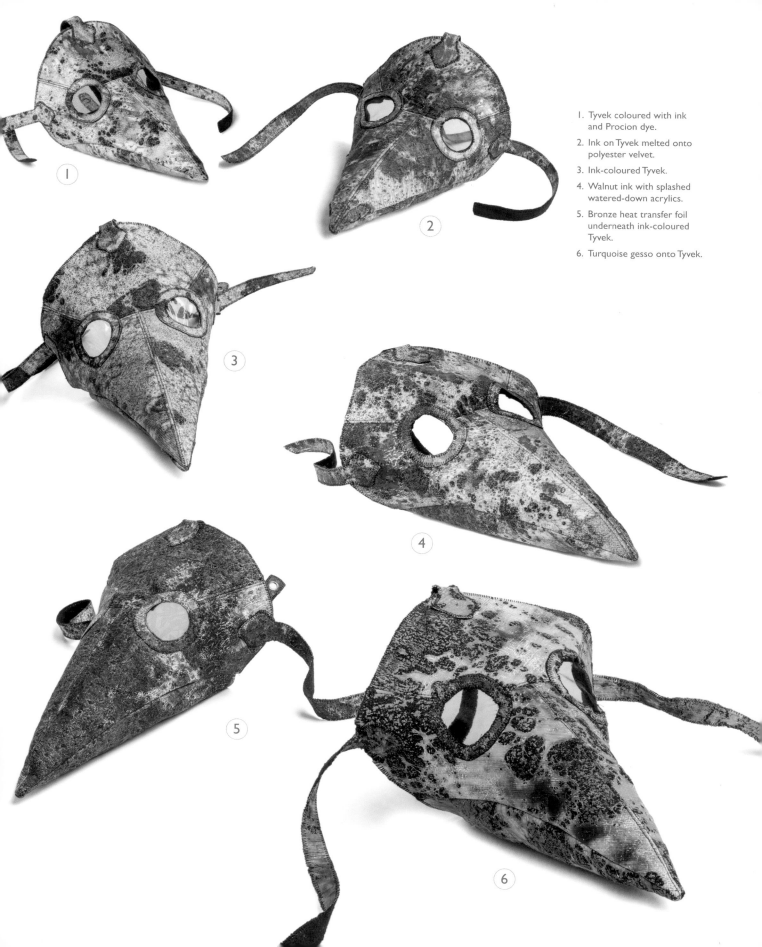

1. Tyvek coloured with ink and Procion dye.

2. Ink on Tyvek melted onto polyester velvet.

3. Ink-coloured Tyvek.

4. Walnut ink with splashed watered-down acrylics.

5. Bronze heat transfer foil underneath ink-coloured Tyvek.

6. Turquoise gesso onto Tyvek.

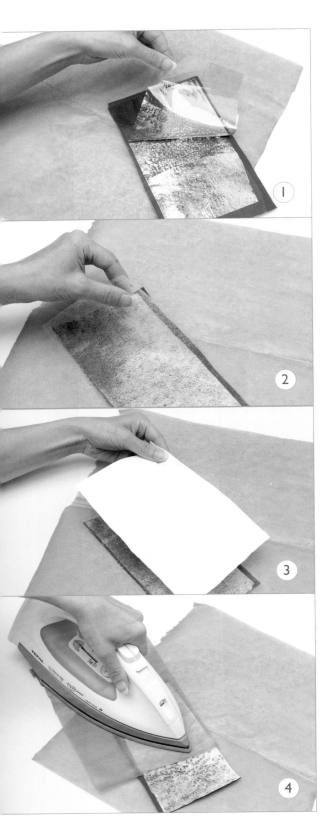

Heat transfer foil

Heat transfer foil can be added underneath the Tyvek before melting, or on the surface after melting.

To add the heat transfer foil underneath the Tyvek:

1. Foil the felt by ironing on a layer of Bondaweb and peeling off the backing paper. Now place the heat transfer foil, colour side facing you, on top of the Bondaweb, cover with baking paper and iron for a few seconds. Make sure the iron is on the warm (wool) setting. If the iron is too hot, the foil will crinkle but will not transfer. Remove the cellophane backing from the foil. You can see in the photo that a hotter iron (on the right of the sample) transfers more foil.

2. Place a sheet of webbing that has been removed from the backing paper onto the foiled surface. Do not iron this sheet of webbing in place.

3. Now place a sheet of Tyvek fabric over the top.

4. Iron the Tyvek, as before. Make sure not to over-iron the Tyvek as it tends to melt far more quickly on a foiled background.

5. You will get more of a distressed look if you scrunch the heat transfer foil first before ironing it onto the felt. This rule also applies if you are going to add the foil after melting the Tyvek.

∧ Heat transfer foil added to the felt before melting the Tyvek fabric on the surface.

> Heat transfer foil added after the Tyvek has been melted.

> Black netting has been added to the surface of this foiled sample.

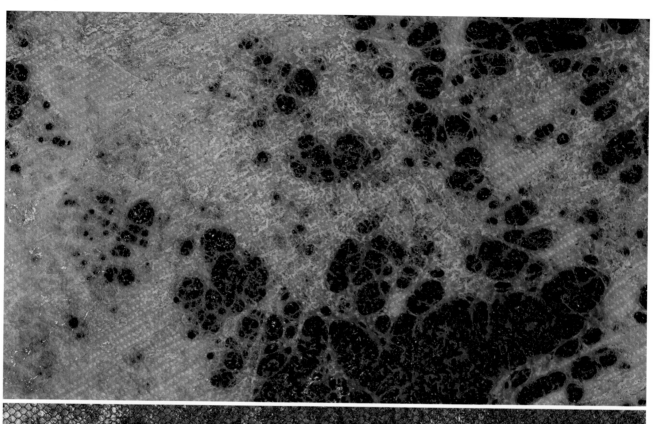

To add the heat transfer foil on top of the melted Tyvek:

1. Make sure your iron is set to the wool setting.

2. Lay the heat transfer foil on top of the surface – no need for fusible webbing or adhesive – and cover with baking paper.

3. Iron very gently for just a few seconds at a time. If you press too hard, you will end up with a solid block of foil and there is a possibility that you may melt the Tyvek further. Keep lifting the baking paper to see what's happening underneath, repeating the process if necessary. Use just the tip of the iron for a small area, or a small iron such as a Clover iron or similar, to apply small areas of foil to the surface.

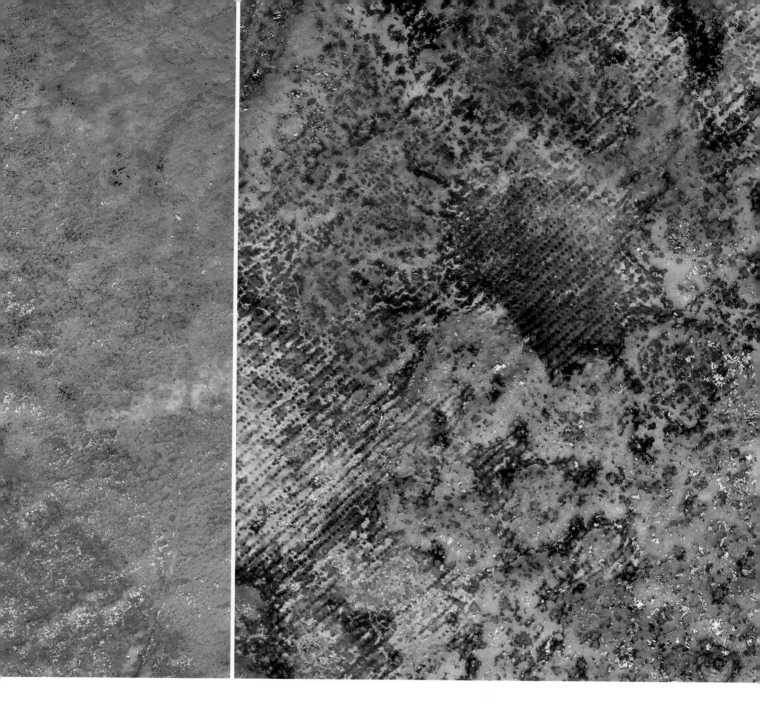

∧ These foiled samples
are white Kunin felt that
has been coloured with
transfer dyes before
melting coloured Tyvek
on the surface.

Trapped threads

This is an ideal way to use up all those snippets of thread.
They can be any threads, knitting yarn or even coloured fleece.

1. Iron fusible webbing onto the felt and remove the
   backing paper.

2. Layer the surface quite thickly with snippets of thread,
   wool or fleece. Have a good covering as when the iron
   presses down, it can leave valleys where the background
   will show through.

3. Lay a further piece of fusible webbing on the top. Do not
   iron this piece down.

4. Now cover with Tyvek and iron in the usual manner.

5. To help any loose threads stay in place, you could cover the
   surface with organza, net or similar, or machine embroider
   into the fabric.

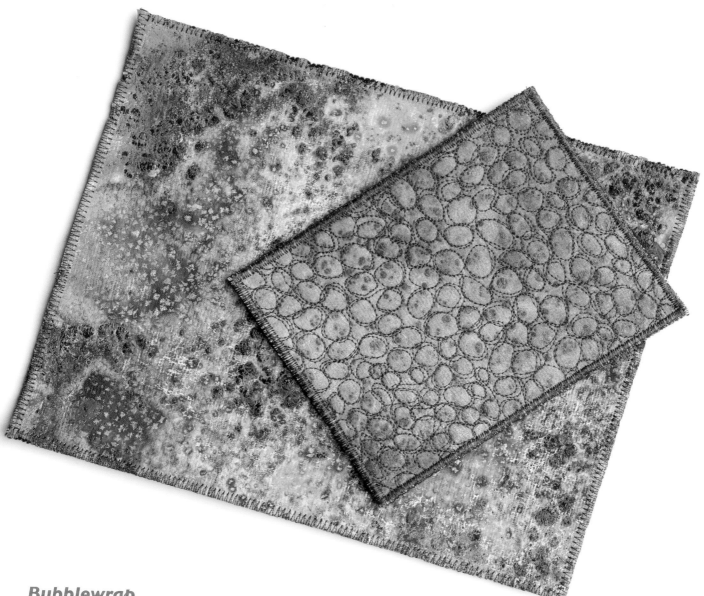

Bubblewrap

Using bubblewrap can add another dimension to your samples.

Iron a layer of fusible webbing onto the felt and remove the backing paper. Lay down the bubblewrap, bubbles facing you, and place the Tyvek on the surface.

Cover with baking paper but, this time, instead of swiping down the fabric with the iron, press hard in one area at a time for just a couple of seconds before moving on to the next area. You should be able to hear the bubbles on the bubblewrap popping as you press the iron down. You will be able to see the outline of the bubbles much more clearly this way.

∧ In the large sample shown here, bubblewrap has been added as an extra layer. The upper piece shows organza which has been stitched on the surface of the bubblewrap.

< Trapped threads.

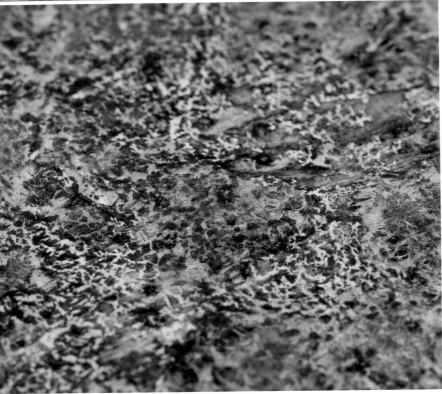

< Glitter flakes added underneath the bubblewrap.

Bubblewrap with glitter flakes

1. Sprinkle the glitter flakes onto the felt. Iron on a layer of fusible webbing.

2. Place the bubblewrap on top, bubbles facing up, and cover with Tyvek.

3. Iron as before, pressing down rather than swiping with the iron.

4. If the glitter flakes remain loose on the surface in some places, after step 2, try ironing another layer of fusible webbing on top of the flakes before adding the Tyvek.

Bubblewrap with trapped threads

Snippets of threads can be trapped underneath the bubblewrap. Here's how:

1. Start by ironing a layer of fusible webbing onto the felt.

2. Lay the threads directly on top and cover with a second layer of webbing. Iron this down as before.

3. Follow this with the bubblewrap, again with the bubbles facing you, before placing the Tyvek on top.

4. Cover with baking paper and press hard with the iron for a couple of seconds before moving on to the next area.

Once completed, you may also wish to iron on the reverse side to make sure the Bondaweb has adhered to the threads sufficiently. Glitter flakes can also be sprinkled onto the snippets of threads to give added interest.

< Trapped threads can be seen underneath the layer of Tyvek and bubblewrap.

Partially melted Tyvek

This sample came about because a student, Jo Walden, had forgotten to place the webbing on top of the felt before melting the Tyvek. To save waste, she still decided to bond the Tyvek to the felt and the result looked so good that it had to be included here.

Place the Tyvek fabric between two sheets of baking paper. Using a hot iron, lightly press the Tyvek until it starts to wrinkle. Try not to go too far or the Tyvek will melt away completely. Now place the melted fabric on top of the webbing and felt, cover with baking paper and iron as before. This will add texture to your sample.

Stitching before melting

Machine stitching the Tyvek 'sandwich' before zapping will give you more control over the melting process.

For random stitching, use a long machine stitch or freehand machine stitch and work through from the front, gently pulling the Tyvek fabric as you stitch to stop it from puckering.

For larger pieces, where definite patterning is required, draw your pattern on a piece of stiffer fabric such as calico, duck cotton etc. and work from the back. To prevent the Tyvek from bunching up, it's a good idea to pin and then tack the pieces together before stitching.

∧ Tyvek fabric partially melted before layering with the fusible webbing and felt.

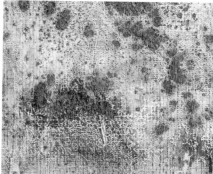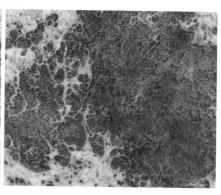

Other fabrics to try

Many more samples can be created by trying the coloured Tyvek technique with different fabrics. Each of them will give you a different result. Most of the fabrics can be foiled before ironing the Tyvek to the surface. Use the same method as before to bond the Tyvek to the fabric.

Polyester velvet on its own tends to ripple, so if you want a smooth surface then bond it to a felt background before adding the layer of webbing and the Tyvek.

It can also be bonded to another fabric such as pelmet Vilene, but the polyester velvet tends to remain flat rather than rising up through the Tyvek.

∧ Polyester velvet makes a great base for coloured Tyvek as you can see from these samples.

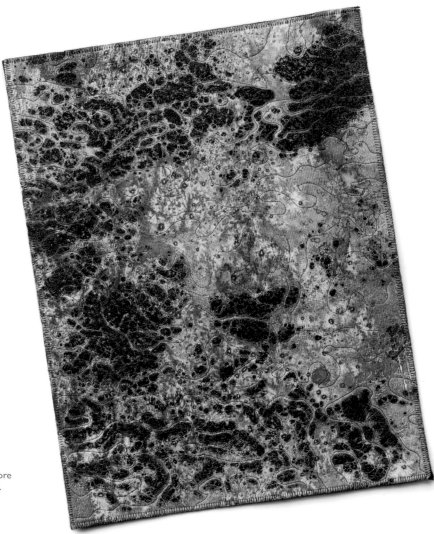

< Steampunk shoulder bags made with coloured Tyvek, coloured felt and polyester velvet.

> This piece has been machine stitched before melting with the iron.

< Steampunk coat and hat. Here, Tyvek was coloured with Quink black writing ink and sprinkled with sea salt. The Tyvek was then bonded to a wine-coloured polyester velvet that was backed with black acrylic felt. The sleeves and collar are polyester velvet covered with black netting. A matching bag is shown above.

Organza has an ethereal look to it. The resulting fabric can be overlaid onto another background to give it substance. The Tyvek fabric tends to melt a lot more quickly on organza so be careful not to over-iron it.

> The top three samples show Tyvek with Organza.

> At the base is a Decovil sample.

Decovil is a fusible non-woven interfacing with a leather-like feel, ideally suited for the creation of hats, belts, bags and small fabric bowls etc. It comes in two different weights – select the weight that is appropriate for your finished creation.

One side of the Decovil already has a layer of fusible webbing attached, so the additional layer of webbing can be omitted. Lay the Tyvek directly onto the sticky side of the Decovil and iron as normal.

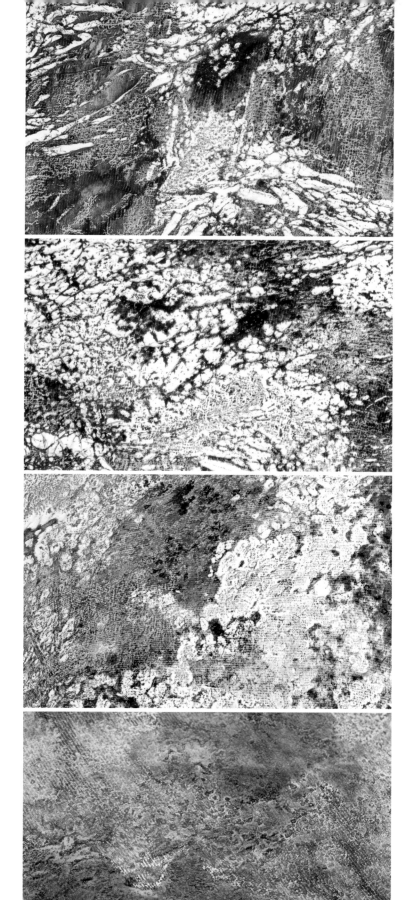

∧ *Vessel.* Heat transfer paints were used to colour the surface of Decovil, with heat transfer foil bonded to the surface. Foil was also used on the sticky underside of the Decovil. Plain white Tyvek fabric was then bonded to the surface before the resulting fabric was cut into an intricate design using a cutting machine. The sides were machine stitched to hold the vessel together.

> To the right you can see the bonded material that was used in the vessel construction.

Decovil, Lutradur and Evolon all benefit from being coloured first before melting Tyvek on the top. These can be coloured with all manner of mediums as you will not be washing the item you are creating. As they are synthetic fabrics, they can also be coloured very successfully with heat transfer dyes.

Care needs to be taken when colouring Decovil as one side is already sticky. You would need to colour the non-adhesive side and add a layer of fusible webbing before applying the Tyvek.

When colouring the Decovil, be sure to lay it on baking paper, with the sticky side down. As soon as you have coloured the Decovil sufficiently, immediately remove it from the baking paper. The hot iron will activate the adhesive and it will stick to the baking paper as it cools if care is not taken.

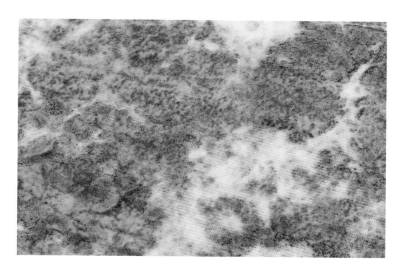

∨ Decovil was random dyed with heat transfer paints. Plain white Tyvek fabric was then bonded to the surface before cutting with a cutting machine to form this lovely casket. Above you can also see a detail of the Decovil fabric that was used to make the casket.

Lutradur is a non-woven polyester material. At first glance, it looks like dressmakers' interfacing but its unique spun woven structure makes it see-through in nature. It comes in a variety of different weights; the lighter the material, the easier it is to see through it.

< Lutradur sample.

< Lutradur with partially melted Tyvek fabric.

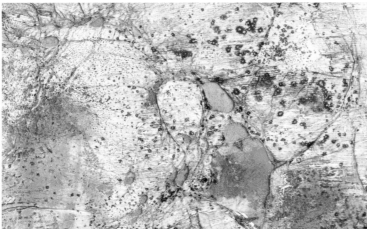

Evolon is a white microfibre cloth made from polyester and nylon. It comes in two different weights and has the touch and texture of fine suede.

< Evolon samples.

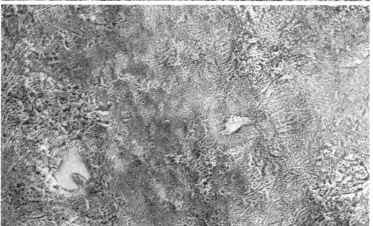

> To create these vintage slippers, Evolon was random dyed with heat transfer paints. Tyvek fabric was coloured with walnut ink, sprinkled with sea salt and splashed with Procion dye, then bonded to the Evolon.

> You can also see the fabric that was used to construct the shoes.

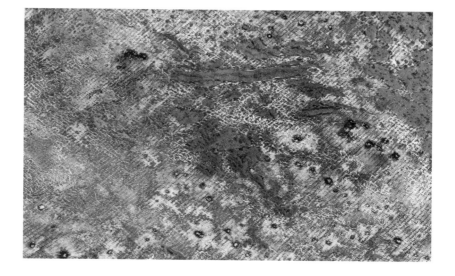

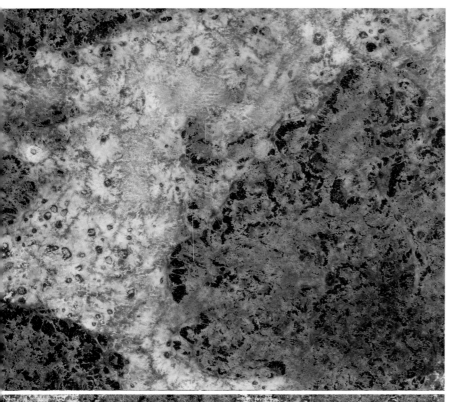

Tyvek paper

Tyvek paper is more sturdy than the fabric variety and is available in three different weights: 55 gsm, 75 gsm and 100 gsm. It works very well for this technique but will have a much stiffer feel than the Tyvek fabric.

< Sample made from Tyvek paper.

< Sample made from wool felt.

Try using wool felt. Although the result will be pretty much the same, bear in mind that you will not be able to use the soldering iron to cut through the fabric.

> Steampunk jacket and hat constructed from fabric created using the basic Tyvek and Kunin/acrylic felt technique. The Tyvek was coloured with walnut ink, sprinkled with sea salt, with turquoise Procion dye splashed on afterwards.

On the surface

Once your new fabric has been created, whether you use Tyvek fabric or Tyvek paper, you can add a variety of top dressings:

- Organza can be laid on top and stitched around the edges or machine stitched to hold it in place.
- Net can be used in the same way or added beneath or above the organza.
- Machine stitching with a decorative pattern gives added interest to the surface.
- Beads can be added for an extra sparkle after any of the stages above.

∨ A clutch bag with net and a die-cut decoration – see page 38 for details of cut outs.

∧ Notebook holders which have organza and net laid, or stitched, on the surface.

Laminated fabric

Laminating the fabric can be useful, especially if the piece is going to take a lot of handling. Use a product called Lamifix. This is available in either matt or gloss. Lay the Lamifix on top of the fabric, cover with baking paper and use a warm iron to fix it to the surface. The resulting fabric can be used successfully for bags and jewellery.

∨ Laminated Tyvek fabric with trapped threads and organza. Note that the top fabric has been foiled.

> Right and below. Samples of laminated fabrics.

< This sample has been laminated and foiled.

> The Tyvek fabric in this hanging has been
  stitched to a felt background before
  applying heat. The leaf shapes have been
  cut from the same background fabric with
  a cutting machine.

∨ Coloured Bondaweb applied on the surface
  of the Tyvek fabric after melting.

  Coloured Bondaweb applied above and
  below the surface of the Tyvek fabric.

Coloured Bondaweb can be added before or
after melting the Tyvek. Colour the Bondaweb
with watered-down acrylic paints, silk paints
or ScolaBrush applied with a sponge and
leave to dry before ironing in the usual
manner. The finished fabric can now
be used in any way you wish. It is
very easy to stitch into or stitch
together and shape.

A soldering iron will slice through the fabric very easily.

Work on a heat-resistant surface. You can use a template to cut around or work freehand. Let the soldering iron heat up, position it in place on the fabric and gently guide it in the direction of your shape, preferably working away from you.

Don't try to pull the soldering iron through the fabric – this is when accidents can happen. Sometimes the temperature of the iron will dip. If this occurs then wait a couple of minutes until it has reheated rather than struggle to cut through the fabric.

The fabric can also be cut using one of the many cutting machines available. A Sizzix Big Shot has been used for these samples along with Tim Holtz dies 'Tattered Florals' and 'Tattered Poinsettias'.

< This vessel has been decorated with leaf shapes that have been cut from the fabric with a soldering iron.

> A selection of flowers cut with a Big Shot machine and Tim Holtz 'Tattered Florals' die.

∧ A selection of brooches cut with a Big Shot machine and Tim Holtz 'Tattered Florals' die. Some of the brooches have been attached to labels made with felt.

To make brooches from these shapes you may like to think about using thick ECO felt for the base layer or even two pieces of felt bonded together. This will make the fabric a lot stiffer.

Laminated fabric can also be cut with a soldering iron or cutting machine.

SECTION 5
Thermofax screens and stencils

Xpandaprint can be applied to the Tyvek either before or after melting using a Thermofax screen. Thermofax screens use a fine polyester mesh with a thin, clear plastic film backing. This is fed into the Thermofax machine along with carbon-based artwork such as laser prints, photocopies, carbon ink or pencil drawings. When the carbon artwork is heated by a Thermofax lamp, the plastic film burns away, leaving the image on the mesh.

Thermofax screens are an alternative way of screen printing onto fabrics and paper. It is a process that is good for reproducing images or marks that would be difficult or expensive using other screen methods.

∨ Foiling using a Thermofax screen and applied to the Tyvek fabric after melting.

> Xpandaprint applied to the Tyvek fabric surface after
melting.

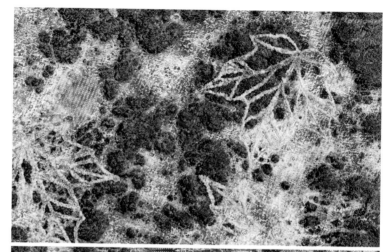

The Xpandaprint is heated with a heat tool
immediately after application. Alternatively, wait
until it is dry and then use a hot iron to puff
the paste. You can also apply the Xpandaprint
before melting the Tyvek. Allowing it to dry and
melting the Tyvek with the iron will also puff the
Xpandaprint at the same time. Full instructions
for the process are shown on page 44.

Puff additive, produced by Jacquard to use with
their screen printing inks, can be applied before
or after melting the Tyvek. Mix up to 10% puff
additive with the screen printing inks, apply and
expand with a heat tool. The heat tool is essential
for this product – an iron will not expand
the paste.

Embossing powder or foiling can be carried out
using the same method. This will need to be
done after the Tyvek has melted, especially in the
case of the embossing powder as the heat of the
iron has an adverse effect on the powder.

> Puff additive printed through a stencil onto the melted
Tyvek fabric surface and heated with a heat tool.

> Why not try using a Thermofax screen or a stencil
to print an actual design with the Xpandaprint or
puff additive?

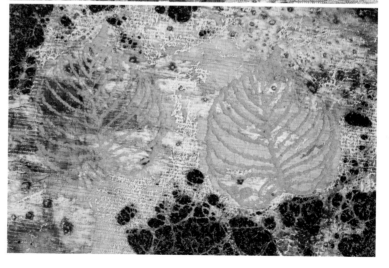

Caring for and using your Thermofax screen

If you feel the screen, you will notice one side feels rough and the other side feels smooth. It is the rough side that should be face-up each time and the smooth side should be on your fabric. Occasional printing through the 'wrong' side (when you want to print a reverse of the design) should not cause any problems but be aware that the smooth side is where the plastic film has been burned away and excess use of the squeegee on the wrong side could tear the edges of the design.

When using mediums with your screen, you will be able to get two or three good prints each time before the design starts to smudge at the edges or the medium starts to dry out. When this happens, the screen must then be cleaned immediately. This is very important. Mediums such as Xpandaprint, gel medium, gesso etc. will block the holes in the mesh if left to dry, making the screen unusable.

These screens will last for a very long time if cared for properly. Keep a cat litter tray or similar filled with water close by. As soon as it is time to clean the screen, wipe away any excess medium with a baby wipe then drop the screen in the water and use a sponge to clean off any residue. Gently pat dry with a cloth and store the screen flat. The duct tape around the edges may start to lift if washed often. Either pull the tape off and replace with new tape or tape over the top. Make sure the screen is thoroughly dry before adding new tape. Store the screens flat at room temperature away from direct light or heat.

Stencils

A stencil is a series of holes cut into a sheet of resilient, waterproof material such as paper or plastic. When paint is applied through the cut-out areas to the surface beneath, an image is formed.

Open sections of the stencil are called islands. These are the areas that allow colour to be applied onto the surface beneath. Bridges are the stencil material that separates the islands and keep the shape. These areas block the paint from reaching the surface.

Mediums can be applied through the stencil in several ways, by using a stippling brush or a sponge, or you could use a squeegee to scrape the medium through (very lightly).

When using mixed-media products with stencils, they will need to be washed frequently before the medium dries on the surface. There is a plethora of designs to choose from when buying stencils – or you could make your own.

Making your own stencil

Temporary stencils can be made from Tyvek, freezer paper or thick card. Coat the card with button polish to keep it waterproof and to make sure it will last a little longer. Stencil acetate can be purchased to make stencils. Use a soldering iron to cut out the shapes. Once again, the stencils will need to be washed immediately after using any mixed media products to ensure that they remain in the best condition.

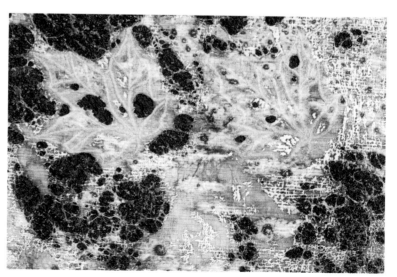

> Xpandaprint applied to the Tyvek fabric surface before melting. Note how it takes up the colour of the surface below.

Applying Xpandaprint or puff additive through a Thermofax screen or stencil

The basic technique:

1. Lay your finished fabric or the coloured Tyvek on your printing surface. Place your screen, right side facing, on the top.

2. Using a palette knife or similar, place a bead of medium, in this example Xpandaprint, along the top edge of the screen.

3. Now pull through with the squeegee. Hold your squeegee at a 45° angle. If the squeegee is too flat, the medium will spread under the screen and the image will look thick and blurred. You want a sharp image. Don't despair if you don't get it right first time – this will take practice.

4. Remove the Thermofax screen from the fabric and wash the screen immediately before the paste has a chance to dry.

5. Move the printed fabric to a heat-protected surface and zap lightly with the heat tool, taking care not to melt back the Tyvek. Alternatively, allow the medium to dry and activate with a hot iron.

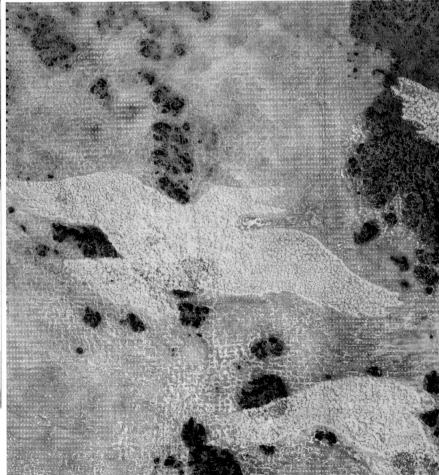

The method for using a stencil
is pretty much the same except
you must be careful to put the
Xpandaprint on as thinly as possible.
If too much Xpandaprint is applied,
you will be left with large pieces
of 'popcorn' when it puffs up. That
will take away the definition of
the design.

> Puff additive used through a Thermofax
screen onto the Tyvek fabric.

∨ Xpandaprint used through a Thermofax
Screen on to the Tyvek fabric. Although the
Xpandaprint was applied directly from the
pot, you can see how it tends to draw up
some of the background colour.

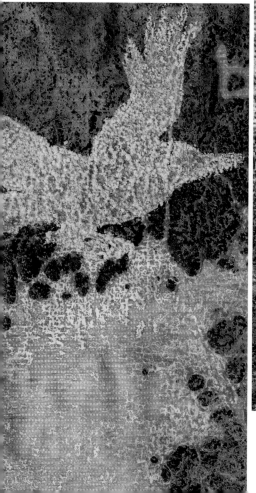

∧ Embossing powder applied to
the Tyvek fabric after melting
using a Thermofax screen.

Embossing powder

To apply embossing powder, use a white glue that dries clear. My preference is matt medium but any of the gel mediums, acrylic wax or découpage glue will work. PVA also works but takes a bit of practice as it can be quite runny. Regular gel medium is a good one to start practising with as it is quite thick and very easy to work. You will need to work quickly as the embossing powder needs to be applied before the glue starts to dry.

Start with a small bead of glue. You really do only need a small amount. Pull the glue down the screen with the squeegee two or three times or until you see that the holes in the mesh have filled. If you haven't applied quite enough glue to fill the holes then just add a little more in the areas that need it. If too much glue is used, it will spread underneath the screen or stencil and will give a blurred image.

Once you have printed your design, place your screen or stencil face down in a bowl of water. This will need to be washed as soon as possible – speed is of the essence here.

1. Place your printed fabric on a sheet of scrap paper and sprinkle the embossing powder all over your design.

2. Lift the fabric and tap off the excess powder onto the scrap paper. This can now be transferred back into the jar.

3. Now heat the embossing powder, using a heat tool on a low heat, until it has embossed.

This technique can only be used after you have bonded your Tyvek to the background.

Applying heat with an iron once you have embossed knocks back the shine of the embossing powder.

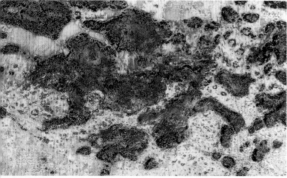

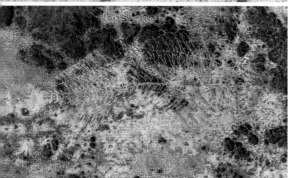

< In these samples foil has been applied to the Tyvek fabric after melting, using a Thermofax screen.

< Screen printing ink applied to the surface and foiled after melting.

Heat transfer foil

Use a white glue through a Thermofax screen or stencil and follow the same instructions as for the embossing powder. Place the heat transfer foil, colour side up, onto the glue and iron very lightly with a warm iron. Use the tip of the iron over the design area or the foil will also be picked up in places on the surface of the Tyvek.

I do hope you will have fun trying some of these techniques. Just remember – there are no failures in mixed-media textiles. If your sample doesn't turn out as you wish, you can carry on layering fabrics and mediums on the surface until you achieve a satisfactory result. Alternatively, you can always cut the piece into smaller sections to incorporate into another piece of work.

Keep everything, throw nothing away, and always make a note of exactly what materials and mediums you have used to obtain that stunning sample.

> Tyvek, coloured with Quink writing ink and melted onto acrylic felt, has been used to cover these hexagonal hat boxes. Bleach has been used through a Thermofax screen to add interest to the surface. There is more about this technique in the free online workshops.

Suppliers

Most of the materials used in this book are listed here. For those that aren't, and for readers outside the UK, go to *www.d4daisy.com* and click on Suppliers (or try Google).

Art Van Go
Most materials mentioned in the book
www.vycombe-arts.co.uk

Lynda Monk
Tyvek fabric by the metre and Thermofax screens made to order
www.purplemissus.com

Rainbow Silks
Kunin felt
www.rainbowsilks.co.uk

Spenic Graphics
Tyvek fabric and paper on rolls. Also in sheets (paper only).
www.spenic-graphics.com

Suzie May Crafts
Acrylic felt, organza and polyester velvet
info@suziemaycrafts.com

Books and websites

d4daisy Books Ltd
Books, information, free classes with some books, glossary
www.d4daisy.com

Workshop on the Web
Internet textile magazine with free taster. Soon to be transformed into a d4daisy book with lots of additional material online.
www.workshopontheweb.com

Michael Wicks Photographer
Specialist textiles photography
www.michaelwicks.com

...also available from www.d4daisy.com

Cut, Shape, Stitch
Maggie Grey
Sam Packer
& Paula Watkins
Explore the world of simple punches & die-cutters through to the latest digital machines
978-0-9574413-2-3

Approaches to Stitch: six artists
Ed. Maggie Grey
Elizabeth Brimelow Ro Bruhn, Ruth Lee, Sian Martin, Olga Norris and Beryl Taylor
978-0-9574413-1-6

Dissolvable Delights
Maggie Grey
Innovative mixed media techniques, majoring on water-soluble materials
978-0-9555371-9-6

Exploring Creative Surfaces
Lynda Monk
Inventive textures with scrim, Tyvek and paint
978-0-9574413-0-9

Fabulous Surfaces
Lynda Monk
From tissue paper to old dressmaking patterns – distress, rust and sculpt!
978-0-9555371-8-9

Long Diaries Tall Tales
Maggie Grey
Maggie works on the theme of story telling using mixed-media to make up a diary of a journey
978-0-9574413-3-0